99 FAVORITE AMISH
Home Remedies

GEORGIA VAROZZA

HARVEST HOUSE PUBLISHERS
EUGENE, OREGON

Cover by Dugan Design Group

Cover photo © Dugan Design Group

99 FAVORITE AMISH HOME REMEDIES

Copyright © 2016 Georgia Varozza
Published by Harvest House Publishers
Eugene, Oregon 97402
www.harvesthousepublishers.com

Library of Congress Cataloging-in-Publication Data
   Varozza, Georgia
   99 favorite Amish home remedies / Georgia Varozza.
      pages cm
   ISBN 978-0-7369-6593-4 (pbk.)
   ISBN 978-0-7369-6594-1 (eBook)
   1. Traditional medicine. 2. Medicine--Formulae, receipts, prescriptions. I. Title. II. Title: Ninety-nine favorite Amish home remedies.
      GR880.V37 2016
      615.8'8--dc23   2015023107

Printed in China

   16 17 18 19 20 21 22 23 24 / RDS-KBD / 10 9 8 7 6 5 4 3 2

To my beloved family—
As always.

ACKNOWLEDGMENTS

Nick Harrison—Your encouraging words and positive attitude started me on my writing adventure. I know I speak for countless others when I say I'm so thankful I listened to you! I love how you can take my disparate thoughts and bring focus to what I'm really trying to get across. Thanks, friend!

Kim Moore—I've been fortunate to have you as my editor. Truly, I've never known anyone with such a gift for detail, and your legendary memory continues to amaze me. You are gracious and kind, and your special box of chocolates has seen me through more than one crisis! It doesn't get any better than you.

The Varozza clan: Walker, Travis, Logan, Sara, Crystal, Audrey, Asher, Easton, Alexis, Everett, Nicole, and Lucas—Without my family, I wouldn't have been as apt to find homemade solutions to life's little difficulties. You guys keep me going!

CONTENTS

COLDS, FLU, AND
ALLERGIES

HEADACHES AND
EARACHES

HOUSE AND YARD

PERSONAL CARE

SALVES, OINTMENTS,
TONICS, AND BALMS

SLEEP ISSUES
AND STRESS

WOMEN'S HEALTH

AMISH REMEDIES ARE GOOD FOR YOU!

The Amish are not averse to taking advantage of modern medical technology, especially in the less conservative groups. Because they do not have formal church rules regarding health care, decisions about what type of medical treatment to use is informally decided by individual communities or within families. The Plain groups more open to change tend to avail themselves of modern medicine sooner and more often than do the more conservative groups. However, alternative methodologies are usually welcome in all communities. The Amish have a stoic sense that illness and injury are part of God's will, and as a result they aren't as quick to run to the doctor as are their English counterparts. Therefore, home remedies play a big part in many communities, especially for minor illnesses or injuries.

Because the Amish have a somewhat condensed and unique gene pool, they are disproportionately affected by certain rare genetic disorders. As a result, families often have astronomical medical bills. Added to this is the fact that most Amish do not participate in any type of health insurance plan, so these hard-hit people are responsible for the sometimes staggering amounts. But, as in every other aspect of Plain life, the community offers tangible support and helps to defray some of the costs by engaging in benefit auctions and sales, as well as collecting regular offerings for the church's mutual aid fund.

So, when comon colds, flu, aches and pains, or anxious times occur, it just makes sense for folks to reach for ingredients in their kitchen cupboards to naturally—and inexpensively—find a cure for what ails them. And for those of us who are interested in self-reliant alternatives to a quick trip to the doctor, the remedies in this book might just prove to be useful and effective for us as well.

The remedies I'm sharing with you in this book have been safely and effectively used by Plain and non-Plain people for generations. These old-fashioned solutions to everyday problems use common items, many of which you probably already have in your cupboards, and what ingredients you don't have you can easily purchase. Even better, if you're a gardener, a lot of these ingredients can be harvested from your backyard. For the most part, you can use what you make right away, but it's a good idea to read through the book and make note of any mixtures that may need to set for a time before using. That way, when injury or illness strikes, you'll be prepared.

Obviously, this isn't an exhaustive collection of cures and solutions for what ails you and your loved ones. Rather, these are a sampling of remedies that have proven useful to me and my family for many years. I hope you enjoy reading *99 Favorite Amish Home Remedies* and that you'll be encouraged to try a few of the recipes. I think you'll be pleased!

COLDS, FLU, AND ALLERGIES

She looks well to the ways of her household,
and does not eat the bread of idleness.

PROVERBS 31:27 NASB

Dear Lord, I pray You would bathe this home in
peace and joy and bind us together in love. Shield
us, Father, from sin and despair, and help us to
always remember that here, in this house, we
can find respite from our daily cares. May our
words to one another be sweet and seasoned with
kindness. May we be quick to offer grace and
slow to anger. Help me, Father, to care well for
my loved ones and point them always to You.
In Jesus' name, amen.

1

Are you coughing or wheezing, or do you have phlegm in your throat? Homemade **horehound cough syrup** will help. Horehound is a member of the mint family and has been used to tame coughs and colds for hundreds of years. You can easily and quickly make this cough syrup. Store it in a clean jar in the refrigerator, and it will keep for about two months.

1 oz. fresh or dried horehound leaves
1 pint boiling water
3 cups honey, more or less

Bring the water to a boil. Add the horehound leaves and then reduce the heat. When you have a gentle simmer, let the mixture steep for 10 minutes. Strain the leaves and measure the amount of liquid. Add twice as much honey as the amount of liquid and mix well. Pour the cough syrup into a sterilized glass jar, cover, and keep it in the refrigerator.

To use: Take 1 teaspoon cough syrup up to 4 times daily.

Note: If you don't have a food scale to weigh an ounce of horehound, that's equivalent to about ¼-⅓ cup ground or ¾-1 cup chopped herb.

Notes:

2

If you have a mild cold, **horehound tea** will help. (This tea is also good in aiding digestion and stimulating the appetite.) Simply steep 1 ounce of fresh or dried horehound leaves in a pint of water.

To use: Heat about 4 ounces of the tea at a time and drink up to four times daily. If you find the aftertaste somewhat bitter, you can add some lemon and honey to your cup of tea.

Note: If you don't have a food scale to weigh out an ounce of horehound, that's equivalent to about ¼-⅓ cup ground or ¾-1 cup chopped herb.

Don't worry about what you could do if you lived your life over. Get busy with what's left.

—AMISH PROVERB

Notes:

3

A **decongestant** can be worth its weight in gold when you're stuffed up and feeling lousy. This remedy has helped clear sinuses for generations.

2 tsp. peppermint leaves, dried or chopped fresh
1 tsp. rosemary, heaping
1 tsp. thyme, heaping
1 quart water

In a saucepan, add the peppermint, rosemary, and thyme to the water. Bring to a boil and then turn off heat and cover the pot, letting the mixture steep for several minutes.

Remove the cover from the pot and then drape a towel over your head. Lean over the pot, making sure the towel tents in such a way that the steam gets caught inside the towel. Close your eyes and breathe in the aroma. Make sure before you get close to the pot that the steam isn't too hot, and don't get so close that the steam burns you. Breathe in for up to 5 minutes and repeat as necessary. The steam helps to moisturize and soothe your nostrils while the herbs are natural decongestants.

Notes:

4

Placing a **garlic plaster** on your chest will help to clear up colds and flu, and it's quick and easy to prepare. Simply mince several garlic cloves and then add olive oil to make a thick paste. Spread this paste on a square of flannel or muslin that's large enough so that you can completely enfold the paste in the cloth so nothing oozes out. Place the square of fabric onto your chest and then cover with a hot water bottle or warmed blankets or towels. Keep the plaster on your chest for about 15-20 minutes.

Growing up, my siblings and I ate a clove of garlic most days during the winter, and we rarely suffered from seasonal colds and flu. Dad would chop the clove of garlic and have us drink it down with a glass of milk or water. He teased us by saying that an added bonus for him was that he was fairly certain it would keep the young men away from us. And with four daughters, he had a big job!

*Faith is like an umbrella. It protects us
through the storms of life.*

—Amish proverb

Notes:

5

If you have stubborn chest congestion, a **mustard plaster** should help loosen things up.

1 T. mustard powder
¼ cup flour
warm water

Mix together the mustard powder and flour and then add just enough warm water to make a thick paste. Put the paste in the middle of a large square of flannel or muslin and then wrap the fabric so that the mustard mixture is covered and can't ooze out. Place the plaster onto the sick person's chest and leave it on for 15 minutes. Make sure the plaster itself doesn't come in contact with skin because it can burn.

(Some folks say that a dab of mustard plaster placed directly on **warts** will do away with them in no time.)

A great deal of what we see depends on what we are looking for.

—AMISH PROVERB

Notes:

6

This all-purpose **cold and flu tonic** takes some advance planning, so it's best to make this remedy before the cold and flu season hits so you're not caught unprepared. Here is what you'll need:

sterilized quart jar with nonreactive, tight-fitting lid (plastic lids work well for this)
½ cup fresh horseradish, peeled and chopped
10 cloves garlic, peeled and minced
1 fresh white onion, diced
½ cup fresh ginger root, peeled and chopped
2 fresh jalapenos, sliced (use gloves when handling)
2 lemons, sliced thin (no need to peel, but wash well)
2 T. dried rosemary
1 T. turmeric
¼ tsp. cayenne pepper
apple cider vinegar
honey to taste

Put all of the ingredients except the vinegar and honey into the quart jar. Add enough apple cider vinegar to cover. Screw on the lid and store the mixture in a cupboard or other dark, cool area for one month, shaking the jar once or twice a day.

At the end of the month, strain out the liquid, pressing the mixture to extract as much liquid as possible. Add honey to taste (it will take a lot of honey). Store in the refrigerator.

To use: Add 2-3 tablespoons of tonic to a cup of hot water, tea, or juice and drink. Repeat 2-3 times daily as needed.

Notes:

7

This is such a tasty treatment that it can hardly be called "medicine." To **soothe a sore throat**, **reduce fevers**, and **relieve the effects of common colds**, all you need is some black currant jelly or jam. You can make a tea as follows:

1 T. black currant jam or jelly
juice of half a lemon (about 1 T.)
1 pint water
sugar or honey to taste

Mix together all of the ingredients in a medium saucepan. Bring the mixture to a simmer, and then reduce heat and keep a very low simmer going for about 5-10 minutes, stirring occasionally. Drink the tea while it's hot, several times a day, until you're feeling better.

Black currants are very tart berries, rich in antioxidants and vitamin C, and they are just plain good for you. But if you're thinking of making your own jam, you may have difficulty finding a black currant shrub in your local garden center (they can carry a fungus that kills pine trees, so many stores don't offer them for sale). Plan to buy a jar of ready-made black currant jam or jelly at your local grocery store instead. Buy black versus red currant jam or jelly.

Notes:

8

White willow bark tea is a surefire **fever reducer** and **anti-inflammatory**. It's also effective for **headache**, **osteoarthritis**, and **menstrual cramps**. In earlier times, folks would chew on willow bark for relief, but later they found that a tea was just as effective, so chewing the bad-tasting bark fell out of favor. White willow bark has salicin, which is very similar to aspirin (salicylic acid), and works the same way. If you are taking medication that requires you to not ingest aspirin or you have surgery scheduled in the near future, you'll want to stay away from this tea. Here's how to make and use it:

1-2 tsp. white willow bark
1 cup water
honey to taste

Place the bark and water in a saucepan (you can double or triple this recipe if you want to make several cups at once) and bring to a boil. Cover the pot and simmer for 10 minutes and then turn off the heat, keeping the pot covered, and allow the bark to continue steeping for 30 minutes.

Strain the tea and add honey to taste. Drink up to 4 cups daily. It will take some time before you find relief, so be patient. On the plus side, the positive effects of drinking the tea will last a good long while.

Notes:

9

This **onion-and-honey cough syrup** is a very old recipe, and it's still in use today because it works. As if that's not reason enough to try it, the ingredients are minimal and most likely in your kitchen at this very moment.

Slice an onion or two very thinly and place the slices evenly in a saucepan. (Don't use aluminum, which is reactive.) Pour in just enough honey to barely cover the slices. Heat the mixture for about 45 minutes to one hour, being careful to keep the heat low enough so the bottom of the saucepan doesn't scorch. Don't strain out the onions. Store the mixture in a covered jar in the refrigerator.

To use: Take a spoonful at a time as often as you need to.

Onions have expectorant, antibiotic, and anti-inflammatory properties, all of which work well to subdue your cough. And of course, honey coats and soothes your throat.

> *A bad habit is like a comfortable bed;*
> *easy to get into, but heard to get out of.*
> —AMISH PROVERB

Notes:

10

Onion-and-sugar cough syrup is similar to onion-and-honey cough syrup, but it needs to be made fresh every day or two as it doesn't store well.

Slice about half an onion, depending on the size. Put a slice of onion in a clean jar and then sprinkle on a goodly amount of granulated sugar. Repeat these layers, ending with sugar. Cover the jar (use a tight-fitting lid) and let it sit for 8-12 hours. You'll notice that the sugar draws liquid from the onion slices, and it's this liquid that you will use for your cough syrup. Store the jar in the refrigerator and use within two days.

To use: Simply swallow a spoonful of the liquid as often as needed. This cough syrup is a good one to use with children, although they may object somewhat to the smell of the onion unless their nose is quite stuffed up. Try to entice a spoonful down them by having them first pinch their nose closed.

Triumph is just "umph" added to "try."

—Amish proverb

Notes:

11

This **cold care tea** is based on **echinacea** root, and will reduce the duration and symptoms associated with the common cold, flu, cough, fever, and sore throat. Mix together the following:

2 parts echinacea (you can use all parts of the plant—leaves, flowers, and root)
1 part peppermint leaves
1 part thyme leaves

To use: Boil 1 cup water and then add 1 tablespoon cold care tea leaves. Turn off heat but leave on the hot burner. Cover and steep for 10 minutes. Strain, add a bit of honey if desired, and drink up to three cups daily until symptoms disappear.

Also called purple coneflower, echinacea attracts butterflies and is an easy perennial plant you can grow yourself. It is quite heat- and drought-tolerant and comes back year after year to star in your garden.

*Some people are making such thorough
preparation for rainy days that they
aren't enjoying today's sunshine.*
—AMISH PROVERB

Notes:

12

Elderberry cold and **flu syrup** is a mainstay in homemade remedies. I use this when I feel the flu coming on and it often deters a full-blown case, but it's also great for soothing coughs and sore throats. And if you don't end up needing it for relief, you can always use the syrup on pancakes!

2 pounds very ripe, stemmed, and rinsed blue elderberries
4 cups water
2½ cups sugar

Mix together the elderberries and water in a large pot. Bring to a boil, simmer gently for 20 minutes, and then let it cool. Press out the berry juice using a fine mesh strainer or cheesecloth. There should be pulp but no seeds. (In fact, the seeds will cause vomiting and diarrhea, so don't skip this important step and do take your time to be thorough.) Return the juice to the pot, add the sugar, and cook over medium-low heat until the juice thickens, stirring often so it doesn't burn on the bottom of the pot. Cover and refrigerate.

To use: Take 2 teaspoons 4 times daily while symptoms persist. Or mix in a cup of boiling water and drink as a tea.

Harvesting elderberries is time-consuming and messy. The juice stains something fierce, so it's a good idea to wear gloves and an apron. (In fact, elderberries make a great dyestuff, which should tell you something.) But on the positive side, elderberries grow wild and the harvest is free. Yes, the berries are very small and you have to pick and pick and pick to get enough for your use, but it's worth the effort. Also, you can freeze excess berries for later use.

Notes:

13

Here's an easy recipe for **mouthwash** and a **sore throat gargle.** Pulverize equal parts dried sage and thyme. I use a mortar and pestle for this, but you can also use a spice grinder if you have one. Place about ⅛ cup of the herb mixture in a quart canning jar, cover with 2 cups apple cider vinegar, and stir. Cover jar and place in the refrigerator for 2 weeks, shaking daily. Strain out herbs and refrigerate to store.

To use: You can use as a gargle for sore throats and fresh breath straight from the refrigerator. Alternatively, you can gently heat the mouthwash before gargling, which can be very soothing when you have a store throat. Just make sure to test the temperature first. You want your gargle to be warm, not hot.

*The only ones you should get even with
are those who helped you.*

—AMISH PROVERB

Notes:

14

This recipe for **molasses-and-vinegar cold syrup** will have you feeling better in no time.

½ **cup molasses**
½ **tsp. butter**
1 **T. vinegar (you can use white distilled or apple cider)**

Simmer ingredients gently until well mixed. Remove from heat, pour into a sterilized jar or other container, and let it cool.

To use: Take ½-1 teaspoon as often as needed. Store in the refrigerator if you won't be using it completely within a few days. If your symptoms last more than 3 days, make a fresh batch to continue using.

Abundant living: Think deeply, speak gently, laugh often, work hard, give freely, pay promptly, pray earnestly, and be kind.

—AMISH PROVERB

Notes:

15

When you have a **sore throat**, these easy **gargles** will have you feeling better in no time.

- Place about ¼ teaspoon of table salt into a drinking glass or cup. Add hot water and stir until the salt has mostly dissolved. Gargle with the salt water (the warmer, the better) and spit out. Repeat this several times and then rinse your mouth if the saltiness bothers you. (You can also add ¼ teaspoon turmeric to this gargle for added benefit.)

- Mix together a teaspoon of lemon juice in ½ cup of hot water. Gargle several times.

- Add 5 shakes of hot sauce or cayenne pepper to a cup of hot water, stir, and then gargle. Depending on how raw your throat is, this could sting, but the capsaicin in the pepper will soon bring relief.

- Add 1 teaspoon of apple cider vinegar to ½ cup of hot water. Gargle several times and then drink the last little bit.

Notes:

16

This homemade **licorice root expectorant tea** will help to loosen and thin mucous, reduce inflammation, and **relieve a dry cough** and tickle in your throat.

1 cup water
2 T. dried licorice root

Boil the water and then add the licorice root. Remove from heat, cover the pot, and steep for 15 minutes. Strain, cool to warm, and then drink the tea. Do this 2 times daily.

Don't confuse licorice root with anise, the flavoring found in licorice candy. The licorice plant is a perennial shrub. You can begin harvesting some of the roots after the third year of growth (or make it easy on yourself and buy some at the local store!).

A well-rounded character is square in all his dealings.
—AMISH PROVERB

Notes:

17

Homemade **pepper-and-honey tea** is another great **expectorant** that will relieve your cold and cough symptoms, and it works especially well to remove mucous from your upper respiratory system. Here's what you'll need:

1 tsp. freshly ground black pepper (try to get a fine grind)
1 cup water
1-2 T. honey, depending on taste

Add the pepper to the water and bring it to a boil. Remove from heat, cover, and let steep for 10 minutes. Strain if there are still bits of pepper in the liquid. Stir in the honey and mix well. Drink a cup twice daily.

An alternative to making fresh tea is to simply chew and swallow (or spit out) 3 peppercorns, two or three times daily.

Procrastination is the thief of time.

—AMISH PROVERB

Notes:

HEADACHES, EARACHES, AND NOSEBLEEDS

*The LORD sustains them on their sickbed
and restores them from their bed of illness.*

PSALM 41:3

*Heavenly Father, thank You for the family and friends
You have brought into my life. They mean so much to
me! Help me to stay close to them so that I can better
know how to pray for any needs they may have. I ask,
Lord, that You would bless each of my loved ones today.
Remind them of Your eternal and perfect love, and help
me to point the way to You when I'm with them. If
anyone is ill, I pray that You would heal them. Touch
them, Lord, with Your healing hand. Thank You that You
always provide what is best for each one of us. Help my
loved ones to trust in You in all ways and for everything.
May they be quick to turn to You for all their needs.
In Jesus' name, amen.*

18

Do you suffer from **headaches** or **migraines**? Eat 2-3 fresh or dried leaves of the **feverfew** plant when you feel a headache coming on. Feverfew is a pretty, feathery perennial that looks similar to chamomile and can be grown throughout most of North America. If chewing on the leaves doesn't sound appealing, strip them off the stem, dry them thoroughly (making sure they don't touch while drying), and then crush two or three leaves into powder. Fill an empty gel cap with the powder of no more than 3 leaves per capsule and swallow. In this way, you can make a large batch at one time so you're prepared when the next headache strikes.

*Forgiveness is better than revenge—and
in the long run a lot cheaper.*
—AMISH PROVERB

Notes:

19

Remember that **diet** can play a part in the frequency and severity of headaches. The most common culprits are foods that contain MSG (monosodium glutamate), chocolate, dairy products, peanut butter, pickled foods, red wine, processed meats (such as lunchmeat, bacon, and hot dogs—look for nitrate-free varieties instead), avocados, onions, bananas, and citrus fruits. If you get headaches often, try keeping a food journal for a while to see if you can discover clues as to what your trigger foods may be.

One way to do great things for Christ is to do little things for others.

—AMISH PROVERB

Notes:

20

Turmeric—the main spice used to make curry—works great for alleviating **headache pain** as well as **pain in your muscles and joints**. It has excellent anti-inflammatory benefits. It would be difficult to get as much turmeric into your system as you would need for pain relief by simply adding the spice to your food, and chances are you would get sick of curry in a hurry! Instead, you can purchase the spice in bulk from a health food or bulk food store and then place it in empty gel capsules (you can buy these at health food stores also). Carefully fill each capsule, tamping gently to settle the powder before topping off to get it as full as possible. Alternatively, you can now buy turmeric capsules by the bottle almost anywhere vitamins are sold, including national chains and big box stores, and the price is very reasonable.

To use: Take three to four capsules three to four times a day. Turmeric helps with **arthritis pain** also.

> *Tact is rubbing out another's mistake*
> *instead of rubbing it in.*
> —AMISH PROVERB

Notes:

21

Soothing **lavender** works to reduce the pain of **stress headaches**. You can add several drops of lavender oil or a large handful of flowers to a pot of gently boiling water and then breathe in the vapors. Drape a towel over your head and use it as a tent to trap the vapors. Or you can mix one or two drops of the lavender oil with a food-grade oil such as olive or almond and pat on your temples or the back of your neck. If your pain is not too great, gently massage these areas for a few moments.

Lavender also works well as a sleep aid because of its calming effects. You can rub a drop or two of lavender oil over your bedding or make a sachet using the flowers and tuck that under your pillow.

One family I know actually strews lavender flowers on their carpets and rugs, and when they walk around the house, the soothing scent is released as the flowers are crushed underfoot. They feel their home is a peaceful haven as a result. (All I can think about, however, is that the floors must always need a good vacuuming!)

Notes:

22

Peppermint tea can give soothing **relief from headache pain,** especially headaches associated with **sinus pressure.** Steep peppermint leaves in a cup of boiled water for about 5 minutes, making sure to cover the cup while the leaves steep. When you drink the tea, take a moment to breathe in the steam from the cup. The peppermint vapors have a high menthol component and will open up your sinuses and increase blood flow, which can help reduce your discomfort. Even though peppermint has a sprightly, bright taste and strong scent, it's a great natural relaxer, so don't hesitate to drink it at bedtime. It will help you go to sleep quicker.

Peppermint tea is also a great panacea for digestive problems and nausea.

A duty dodged is like a debt unpaid. It is only deferred,
and we must come back and settle the account at last.

—AMISH PROVERB

Notes:

23

This simple fix can have you headache-free in no time. If you splay your fingers, you'll notice the shape of a *V* that is made by your thumb and index finger. Just **pinch this web of flesh** and hold, using moderate pressure, for about two minutes. Either hand will work well, so take your pick—or better yet, pinch both hands at the same time. You can also take a turn on each hand.

24

Another great trick for getting rid of **headache pain** fast is to **massage** the greater occipital nerve, which is located in the base of your skull at the back of your neck. Use your fingertips (I find that only using one hand at a time works best for me) and massage using a circular motion. It's even more relaxing if someone else does the massaging for you, but you can do a creditable job yourself. And if you add a dab of lavender oil, you'll feel even better.

Notes:

25

A few drops of warm olive oil in the ear will often alleviate the pain of **earaches**.

Place a small amount of olive oil in a heat-proof container and set the container in a larger container or saucepan filled with hot water until the oil is warm but not hot. Check the temperature of the oil carefully—you don't want to burn the ear canal. Tilt the person's head so the ear that needs the oil is pointing up. Use an eye dropper (if you have one) and squeeze 2-3 drops of the warm oil into the ear and then cover loosely with a cotton ball. If you don't have an eye dropper, you can use a Q-tip. Simply drench the cotton end of the Q-tip with enough oil so it will drip into the upturned ear. In a pinch, you can even use your hand. Simply dip a clean finger into the oil and then let the oil drip off the tip into the ear.

Once you have the ear covered loosely with the cotton ball, it's a good idea to have the person lie down for a time with that side up so the oil can work its way down into the ear canal. Warm olive oil is very soothing for earaches and can be used on children. I can well remember my father using this homemade remedy on me when I was a very young child, and I also remember that it always made my earache go away.

Notes:

26

A warm onion poultice works wonders for **stuffed up ears**. Thinly slice or chop an onion or two and gently heat the pieces. (I use a small, preheated, cast iron sauté pan that is well seasoned so the onions don't burn while heating.) Once the slices or pieces are quite warm and a bit mushy, wrap a small amount in several thicknesses of cotton fabric, such as muslin, and then hold the wrapped poultice packet on your ear.

This is an especially good nighttime remedy because the stuffiness in the ears will begin to loosen, possibly causing the patient a more restful sleep. And the warmth is certainly soothing.

A happy home is not without problems, but one that handles them with love and understanding.

—AMISH PROVERB

Notes:

27

If you suffer from **plugged ears**, try gently wiggling the ear to pop the Eustachian tubes. The action of wiggling the ear is similar to what sometimes happens when you exaggerate a yawn—it will open the Eustachian tubes and allow fluid trapped in the ear to drain. Simply grab the ear lobe and gently pull and wiggle. If the ear pops, have the person lie down with that ear closest to the pillow so gravity can aid in getting the fluids to drain out of the ear.

You can wiggle your ears as often as you feel the need. Just be careful to do it gently.

Snowflakes are one of nature's most fragile things, but just look at what they can do when they stick together.

—AMISH PROVERB

Notes:

28

When you have a **nosebleed**, give one or more of these remedies a try.

- Pinch the soft part of your nostrils shut and apply pressure for 10 minutes.

- Roll up a square of gauze into a log. Put it under your upper lip on your gums and press gently until the bleeding stops. You can also use a square piece from a brown lunch or grocery store bag to make the log.

- Use an ice pack made from crushed ice. Place it across the bridge of your nose while pinching your nostrils. This is especially good for nosebleeds that are the result of injury as the ice will help to reduce swelling and bruising.

- Soak a cotton ball or cloth with white vinegar and plug your nostril until the bleeding stops.

A mother's patience is like a tube of toothpaste. It's never quite gone.

—AMISH PROVERB

Notes:

29

This homemade remedy works well for **dry nose**.

1 cup warm water
½ tsp. salt
½ tsp. baking soda

Mix the ingredients together.

To use: Fill a bulb syringe with some of the mixture (you can find these—called nose bulbs—in the baby section of pharmacies and in many grocery stores). Leaning over the sink, gently squeeze the mixture into each nostril, irrigating the inflamed tissue. Repeat with remaining mixture.

God without man is still God. Man without God is nothing.
—AMISH PROVERB

Notes:

HOUSE
AND
YARD

She gets up while it is still night;
she provides food for her family…
She sets about her work vigorously;
her arms are strong for her tasks.

PROVERBS 31:15,17

Dear Lord, I want to be a strong and godly woman, a
woman who follows You always. Help me to daily be
in Your Word and diligent in prayer. Lord, I pray You
would cause me to joyfully care for my loved ones—
to do my best for them always. Help me to work
industriously, keeping in mind that my work can be
a glorious reflection of You. Toward that end, Lord, I
pray that You would make my arms strong for the tasks
at hand, and I thank You that You are with me and
my loved ones and that You never leave us or forsake
us. What an encouragement that is to do my best!
In Jesus' name, amen.

30

Put **bay leaves** in your bags of flour, cornmeal, and biscuit mix to **keep pests out**. Tape bay leaves inside your kitchen pantry, cupboards, and drawers to keep away weevils, ants, and silverfish. Just remember to change the leaves about three times a year to maintain their freshness and pest-repelling odor. Bay leaves are cheap (or you can grow your own and save even more), effective, and totally safe around your food and family.

The moment you're waiting for may never arise. The one you just missed will never return.

—AMISH PROVERB

Notes:

31

You can make a simple **multipurpose cleaner** and **ant deterrent** that will disinfect many surfaces and help keep ants at bay. Wash and peel about 6 or 7 oranges and place the peels in a clean quart jar almost to the top. (Save the orange slices to eat later or juice them.) Pour white vinegar into the jar, covering the peels. Cover with a tight-fitting lid and let the mixture set for a week to 10 days. Strain the liquid into a spray bottle. The citrus scent will infuse the vinegar and the oil from the peels will help to brighten while it cleans.

Use full strength to deter ants. Spray along baseboards and in any areas where you know ants can get into your house. If you find an anthill, pour the mixture down the hole. In households where a lot of citrus is used, you can simply save the peels and strew them at the base of your outside foundation to help repel ants from entering your home.

As a cleaner, you can dilute the mixture using two parts of the vinegar to one part water, although I dilute it further when I wash my wood floors. I use about $1/8$ cup of the vinegar mixture in 2 quarts water.

It's also great on counters and stovetops and even cuts grease when used full strength. But do remember to use a wet cloth to rinse afterward.

Notes:

32

If you've ever suffered an ant invasion, you'll appreciate this homemade **ant killer**. This will work on those small "sugar" or "grease" ants. Here's what you'll need:

quart jar with tight-fitting lid (canning jars work great)
2 cups boiling water
½ cup sugar
1½ T. Borax
small lids, such as from gallon milk jugs or peanut butter or
    mayonnaise jars
cotton balls

Pour boiling water into the jar. Stir in the sugar and Borax until completely dissolved and then let it cool.

To use: Soak cotton balls in liquid and place the cotton in the jar lids. Make sure they are thoroughly wet. Place the lids along known ant pathways. Within 24 hours the ants should have found the liquid. But if they don't seem interested, add a small amount of vegetable oil to the cotton balls. (Sometimes ants prefer grease rather than sugar.) Replenish the liquid as it dries out. If you think no ants have visited your lids, move them to other spots.

Notes:

33

To **clean grout**, make a thick paste with baking soda and either water or hydrogen peroxide. Rub the paste onto the grout and let it set for about five minutes. Then scrub with a stiff toothbrush until it looks clean. Rinse the grout well to get any remaining paste off the surface and then dry with an absorbent towel.

For a modern twist, try using an electric toothbrush. You often find disposable, battery-powered toothbrushes for less than five dollars on sale. The fast action of the electric toothbrush will make short work of your scrubbing time.

34

To **clean grimy wood**, such as kitchen cupboards, mix together one part vegetable or olive oil to two parts baking soda. (You can eyeball the amounts instead of carefully measuring.) The paste will be thick and somewhat dry. Gently scrub, going with the grain of the wood, using your fingers or a toothbrush. The paste will tend to fall off as you scrub, so place a paper towel underneath to catch the bits that drop. Wipe with a soft cloth to remove the last traces of the paste. The oil will make the wood shine, and the baking soda will remove the gunk.

Notes:

35

For years, homemade lye soap scraped into thin slivers was often the only **laundry soap** available. Here's another homemade solution—one that's proven its worth for many years as well. This laundry soap is easy to make and the ingredients are inexpensive.

1 bar Fels-Naptha, Zote, Ivory, or homemade soap
1 cup Borax
1 cup washing soda (this is caustic, so handle with care)

Grate the bar of soap as fine as you can manage. (I use a sturdy zester/grater.) Mix the grated soap flakes with the Borax and washing soda. If you want a finer-textured mixture (which dissolves easier and stays mixed better), you can whir it in a blender or food processor. Just make sure that you let the contents completely settle in the container before opening the top—you don't want to breath in the particles. Store in a canning jar or other container that has a tight-fitting lid.

To use: Add one tablespoon (two or three tablespoons for extra-dirty loads) to the washer as it's filling up and swish to dissolve and mix the soap with the water before adding the load of laundry. A cup of white vinegar in the rinse cycle will help the clothes release all the soap and make them soft, fluffy, and clean.

Notes:

36

If you decide to use homemade laundry soap for your clothes-washing needs, why not try homemade **fabric softener** as well? Here is what you'll need:

1 cup baking soda
1 cup vinegar (use white distilled)
2 cups cold water

In a very large bowl or stainless steel pot, add the baking soda and then pour in the vinegar—the mixture will instantly begin to bubble (hence the very large container). Next, add the cold water and stir to mix. When the mixture settles and stops bubbling, pour it into a large canning jar (half gallon is better than quart) or other container and store tightly sealed.

To use: Before each use, shake the container to combine all ingredients and then add ¼ cup of mixture to your rinse water.

Note: Although I haven't personally tried this addition, you could try adding some drops of essential oil to the liquid fabric softener to give your laundry a fresh and pleasant scent.

Notes:

37

Here's an easy and economical way to make **liquid soap** that works for both hands and dishes.

1 bar Ivory soap
8 cups very hot water

Finely grate the bar of soap. (Or grind it finer in a food processor or blender.) Add the hot water and whisk until the soap is melted. That's it! (Feel free to cut the recipe in half because making a quart at a time is easier to store. Just use a wide-mouth quart-sized canning jar.)

This recipe is rock-bottom cheap, but sometimes when it sets up it's too thick to use in a pump-action soap dispenser. So I store mine in a wide-mouthed quart canning jar with a plastic lid. (A plastic container would work just as well and wouldn't be breakable.) When I'm doing some dishes, I scoop out a few spoonfuls and swish them into the wash water, or I put a small amount on my scrub sponge. Depending on how much it has thickened, I may add more water into the storage container and stir to make sure it's completely incorporated.

Not only can you use this as hand soap, but in a pinch it will also work as a great shampoo. Just be sure to rinse your hair well when you're finished shampooing and then add a vinegar rinse afterward by mixing together ¼ cup white or apple cider vinegar in a quart of warm water and pouring over your hair.

Notes:

38

Your **garden** will benefit from the regular use of **Epsom salt**. You can buy Epsom salt (which is a naturally occurring mineral mixture of magnesium and sulfate) in grocery stores and drugstores, and a box or bag is very inexpensive.

HOUSE AND YARD

- Before planting your vegetable garden in the spring, scratch in one cup of Epsom salt for every 100 square feet of planting area.

- Mix one tablespoon of Epsom salt for every foot of plant height in a watering can for all of your veggies except sage. Repeat as often as every two weeks.

- When planting roses, scratch in a tablespoon or two around the base of the rosebush. Repeat several times during the growing season.

- Fruit will taste sweeter when you use a dilute solution of Epsom salt to water your garden. Use about a quarter of a cup of Epsom salt mixed with plenty of water per 500 square feet. Repeat as often as every two weeks.

- Use two tablespoons of Epsom salt mixed with a gallon of water as a foliar spray for tomatoes, peppers, and eggplants. Your vegetables will be larger and more abundant.

Notes:

39

Have **unsightly weeds?** Here are some easy-to-use ideas to get rid of them.

- Pour boiling water on them. This is in some ways the safest type of weed control because water won't change the pH balance in your soil or leave behind toxic elements that may continue killing any plants that go into that part of your garden. However, if you have a long walk from your boiling water source to the garden, the water can cool enough that it's not always effective, especially on tough weeds. Still, it's worth a try.

- Sprinkle table salt on weeds where they are hard to pull, such as in sidewalk cracks and at the bottom of walls or fences. The salt will kill the weeds quickly. In fact, you should start seeing them begin to wilt by the next day. But don't put salt on your garden areas because your plants won't survive any better than the weeds do.

- Douse weeds with vinegar. Fill a spray bottle with white vinegar and soak the weeds well. Repeat after top watering or rain. Remember that using vinegar will change the pH of the surrounding soil, so use sparingly in garden areas and target just the weeds themselves. You can also add a squirt or two of dish soap for a bit of additional weed-killing power.

- Rig up a small propane tank with a tube and nozzle that can withstand flame, and then burn your weeds. Keep in mind that you'll burn anything if you hold the flame too

Notes:

long in any one spot (think wooden fence slats). You can also buy a weed burning torch that has everything you'll need except for the propane tank to get going quickly and save yourself the hassle of fabricating the item from scratch (especially good if you're not mechanically inclined). This works super well, but it can be a bit pricey. Still, it's a dandy fix if it's within your budget.

40

Believe it or not, black tea makes an excellent **cleaner for wood** and **wood laminate floors**. You can buy inexpensive black tea (bags) and have a dandy floor cleaner for pennies. You can even use flavored black tea if that appeals to you, but usually plain black tea is the least expensive.

Use 3 tea bags in a quart of water that has come to a full rolling boil. (I use a stainless steel pot to make the tea and then dump it into a bucket when it's ready to use.) Steep the tea until it looks good and strong, about 10 minutes. Remove the tea bags and allow the tea to cool enough that it won't burn your hands when you use it.

Use the tea full strength. Be sure to thoroughly soak your mop head (hardwood floor mops with reusable cotton pads work well) or wash rag (if doing your floors by hand) and then squeeze out the excess tea so your floors don't become waterlogged. When the mop head or rag becomes dirty, rinse in clean water (not in the tea!), squeeze out the excess, submerge the mop in the tea, and continue mopping.

The tannins in the black tea will clean and brighten the wood and leave your floors clean and shining!

Notes:

41

Many folks believe that painting the underside of your porch ceiling sky blue will **confuse mud daubers** and **other insects** and they won't be as likely to take up residence near your doors.

In generations past (before the advent of our modern paint mixtures) homemade milk paint or whitewash were used (often with pigments added, such as sieved dirt, cow's blood, or laundry bluing to make colored paint). Whitewash included hydrated lime (a caustic substance), and some hold to the thinking that this ingredient was the cause of keeping the insects at bay. But whether or not it's actual fact, painting porch ceilings blue to keep away insects became common, and many people today swear by the efficacy of that particular color. I've known several people over the years who assured me that their porches stayed much cleaner as a result of that blue paint. If you decide to join the ranks, you may be pleasantly surprised—and at the very least you'll certainly have a lovely porch!

*The key to contentment is to realize
life is a gift, not a right.*
—AMISH PROVERB

Notes:

42

Don't throw out your used **coffee grounds**! Instead, use them in your garden.

- Coffee grounds help deter slugs and snails because they don't like to crawl over the sharp particles. You can make mounded rings around your vulnerable plants to keep pests at bay.

- Spread used coffee grounds around acid-loving plants, such as blueberries, rhododendrons, hydrangeas, camellias, azaleas, and gardenias. They'll show their appreciation by flowering profusely. Coffee grounds aren't terribly acidic because the acid is mostly dissolved in the coffee-making process. Still, they benefit a wide range of plants and vegetables.

- Coffee grounds raked into the top six inches of soil will give a nitrogen boost to your vegetables. The grounds also aid in the tilth of your soil. You can use up to about 1 part grounds for every 3 parts soil, although you'll experience benefits using less than that ratio.

- Seedlings also benefit from the nitrogen boost available from used grounds. You can sprinkle a few grounds into the seedling trays or water them in a solution that you have made by adding some grounds to your watering can.

- You can add your used coffee grounds—filter and all—to your compost pile as a substitute for nitrogen-rich manure, which some people worry could contain pathogens.

Notes:

43

Aphids and mealybugs can wreak havoc on your houseplants. Both leave behind a white, cottony substance on leaves and stems of plants. Mealybugs especially can be tough to conquer, but before you throw out your houseplants, try this first.

Mix together 1 part rubbing alcohol to 3 parts water. Add a drop or 2 of liquid dish soap (the kind that doesn't contain bleach). Mix thoroughly. Using a soft cloth, Q-tip, or cotton ball, gently wash the leaves and stems of your infected plant. Repeat every few days until infestation is eradicated.

44

Mold and mildew can become a problem with your **houseplants**—especially if they get too much water and don't have good air circulation around them. To remove mold, wet a paper towel and wring out excess moisture. Gently wipe leaves, changing your wet paper towel for new ones as needed. Next, scoop out the top layer of soil in the pot and replenish with fresh potting soil. Finally, sprinkle cinnamon on top of the soil. Cinnamon won't hurt your plants, and it will help keep fresh outbreaks of mold at bay.

Now that your potted plant has a fresh start, keep mold away by regularly removing spent blooms and dead leaves. Don't allow the pot to sit in a tray of water, and keep the soil on the dry side.

Notes:

45

We all love to spend time outdoors during the warm months of summer. But with the wonderful weather comes the scourge of mosquitos. This homemade **mosquito trap**, placed near the areas where you spend your time, will help keep those pesky insects to a minimum. Here's what you'll need:

2-liter plastic soda bottle, empty and lid removed
1 cup warm water
¼ cup brown sugar
¼ tsp. yeast (the kind you use when making bread)
Strong black tape (such as electrical tape)

Cut the soda bottle in half. In the bottom half of the bottle, mix together the water, brown sugar, and yeast. Take the top half of the soda bottle and place it inside the bottom half, top side down, making sure that the top of the bottle is immersed in the liquid but does not touch the bottom of the bottle. (You want the mosquitoes to be able to fly into the liquid.) Secure the 2 halves of the bottle with the tape and then continue wrapping the bottle to cover as much of it as possible while leaving the top open. Set the trap in areas where you know mosquitoes will find it…and they will! Make new traps as the old ones fill up.

Notes:

46

Chigger bites can itch something fierce. As soon as you realize you have encountered chiggers, take a hot shower and scrub well to get any remaining creatures off your body. They like to congregate in areas where your skin is thinner, such as your ankles, behind your knees, and the inside of your arms, for example, so take extra care when washing those areas.

To **relieve the itch from chigger bites**, mix together some Vicks VapoRub and table salt to make a soothing ointment. You want to make sure you have a few grains of salt directly on each bite for the best relief. Keep the ointment on as long as possible (it has a tendency to rub off), and reapply as needed.

Experience is a hard teacher. She gives the test first and the lesson afterward.

—Amish proverb

Notes:

47

Here is a surprisingly effective treatment for **ridding your home of fleas**.

Right before bedtime, set a small desk lamp on the floor. (Somewhere on your carpet is better than on bare floors because fleas tend to hide in carpets and rugs.) Pour some water into a bowl (a bowl that is low and wide works well because there is more surface area for fleas to jump into) and squeeze in several squirts of liquid dish soap.

Turn on the lamp and set the bowl of soapy water directly in the light's glow. Keep the lamp on all night, and in the morning you should have dead fleas in the bowl of soapy water.

During the day, generously sprinkle Borax throughout your carpets and rugs. (Make sure pets aren't around!) Let the Borax set for at least an hour and then vacuum thoroughly.

Repeat this process morning and evening for several days.

Deal with the faults of others as gently as you do your own.

—Amish proverb

Notes:

48

Pet dogs and cats usually mean fleas to contend with. Use this **lemon flea spray** to help keep fleas off your pet's coat.

Cut 2 lemons into small pieces. Boil them in 1 quart water (cover the pot) for an hour. Remove from the heat and allow the mixture to steep overnight. In the morning, strain the mixture and pour the liquid into a spray bottle.

To use: Spray your pet thoroughly, avoiding its eyes, nose, and inside of ears. Massage into your pet's fur down to the skin.

49

If you add this homemade **dog and cat flea control** to your pet's diet, fleas won't be so apt to make their skin home.

- Add ½ teaspoon brewer's yeast to your cat's food daily.
- Add ½ teaspoon brewer's yeast and ¼ teaspoon garlic powder to your small dog's food daily (for dogs 30 pounds and less).
- For larger dogs, use 1 teaspoon brewer's yeast and ¼ teaspoon garlic powder.

As these substances get into your pet's system, fleas will stay away.

Notes:

50

If your dog or cat has a **bite wound** or **tender paws** from picking up a burr or sliver, try this remedy that uses calendula flowers.

If there is a foreign object in the paw area, carefully remove it (try using tweezers). Next, bathe the wound area using warm, soapy water. Clip the fur around the wound if necessary.

Apply calendula flower petals to the wound site and loosely cover with gauze or strips of muslin to hold in place. Or use a sock on your pet's paw to keep the petals in place.

51

When your pet suffers from **diarrhea**, you can help. Don't feed them for 24 hours, but make sure they have continuous access to clean water.

When you introduce food back into their diet, start by mixing equal parts of cooked rice and unseasoned cooked chicken or hamburger. For cats and old or smaller dogs, you might have to grind the food. Use a coarse blade on your meat grinder or pulse it in a food processor to make the food particles small enough for them to safely eat.

Continue feeding your pet this bland diet until their diarrhea is gone—usually no longer than 2 days.

Notes:

52

Dogs especially, but cats too, can get **ear mites**. You can usually tell when your pet has an ear mite infestation because their ears will look dirty, with bits of debris inside their ear canals, and the tissue in the inner ear will look red and inflamed. They tend to scratch their ears and will often shake their head or tip it and flatten their ears. Ridding your pet of ear mites isn't a quick process, but diligence will be rewarded.

Soak cotton balls in mineral oil and thoroughly swipe the inside of your pet's ears. Use several cotton balls per ear (one at a time), and massage the ear after swiping. (Your pet will more than likely want to shake their head vigorously after you clean the ear, which is fine.) Repeat this process every 2 or 3 days for an entire month, as it takes that long to be certain that all ear mites have completed their life cycle and been eradicated.

A clear conscience is a soft pillow.

—AMISH PROVERB

Notes:

53

The stench from a dog that has tangled with a skunk is virtually unbearable for both the dog and its owners, and it seems as though that awful smell lingers for weeks and even months. But if you use this homemade **skunk wash**, man's best friend should be smelling sweeter in a hurry.

1 16-oz. bottle hydrogen peroxide
1 cup water
¼ cup baking soda
1 tsp. Dawn dish soap

Mix together the hydrogen peroxide, water, and baking soda and stir until the baking soda is dissolved. Add the Dawn dish soap and gently stir to mix. Place the mixture in a squirt bottle.

To use: Squirt or pour the skunk wash onto your pet's coat and, using your fingertips, massage the liquid into the fur all the way to the skin. Be thorough and try not to miss any areas, but do keep it away from your dog's eyes, nose, and ears. Let the skunk wash set on your pet for 15 minutes and then rinse well.

Note: You may need more than one bottle to make a batch large enough to completely soak your dog's fur depending on its size.

Notes:

PERSONAL
CARE

Do you not know that your bodies are
temples of the Holy Spirit,
who is in you, whom you have received from God?
You are not your own; you were bought at a price.
Therefore honor God with your bodies.

1 Corinthians 6:19-20

Heavenly Father, I know one way to honor You is to take
care of my body and to see to the health and well-being
of my loved ones. Thank You for the task You have set
before me! I take it on gratefully and humbly. And yet,
Lord, I know that even more important to You is my inner
beauty—the beauty that comes from knowing You. As I
spend time in Your Word and in prayer, I am reminded
that You, gentle Shepherd, lead Your sheep. Help me,
Father, to come to You in prayer, knowing that whatever
I ask, if it is Your will, then surely You will provide.
In Jesus' name, amen.

54

Making your own **shampoo** is easier—and cheaper—than you probably think. Just mix together the following ingredients and store in a squeeze bottle, plastic container, or even an empty shampoo bottle. This makes about half a cup of shampoo, but you can double the recipe if you have several people who will be using it.

¼ cup liquid castile soap
¼ cup water
1 T. honey
2 T. lemon juice
½ tsp. vegetable oil (optional, but it's great if you have dry hair)

Apply to wet hair and rinse, just as you would with store-bought shampoo. If you want extra shiny hair, rinse a second time with a bit of white vinegar mixed with water, and then plain water to end.

If scent is something you appreciate, you can add ⅛ teaspoon essential oil, or buy liquid castile soap that is already scented.

PERSONAL CARE

Notes:

55

Probably the easiest way to get **clean hair** is to follow this two-step process:

1. Use some liquid castile soap or rub a bar of Ivory soap over your wet hair and work up a lather. You will need to get every square inch of your scalp and hair soapy, because if you miss a place, that section won't get clean like it would if using a detergent-based shampoo. It's a good idea to let the lather sit on your head for several minutes, so this might be a good time to soap the rest of your body with that bar of Ivory. Then rinse well. You will notice your hair feels as though the soap isn't completely gone, and it will be tangled (although the castile soap rinses out better).

2. Now you're ready for the second step, which is to pour on a vinegar rinse. Use ¼ cup of vinegar (white or apple cider) mixed with a quart of warm water. Pour it over your head and rinse as usual. This gets the remaining soap residue out and makes your hair more manageable.

Notes:

56

Getting rid of **dandruff** can be difficult, but try this homemade remedy:

½ cup oregano, fresh or dried and coarsely chopped
½ cup lavender buds, fresh or dried and coarsely chopped
2 cups apple cider vinegar

Place the oregano and lavender buds into a sterilized wide-mouth quart canning jar, add the apple cider vinegar, and gently push down the herbs to release the air bubbles that are clinging to the herbs. Your goal is to completely cover the herbs with the vinegar. Next, cover the jar tightly with a plastic lid. (Or you can use the two-piece metal lids that come with canning jars, but first cover the top of the jar with plastic wrap or wax paper to keep the metal from coming in contact with the vinegar and corroding.) Store the container away from light for about 10 days and then strain out the herbs before using.

To use: Shampoo and rinse your hair as usual. Mix together 2 tablespoons of the vinegar-herb solution and 1 cup warm water. Pour over your clean hair and massage into scalp. Don't re-rinse your hair.

Notes:

57

Alcohol or witch hazel works as a **deodorant**, and either is easy to use because there's no mixing involved. Use either 99 percent isopropyl or 95 percent grain ethyl alcohol—but remember that if you have freshly shaved underarms, the alcohol will sting. Witch hazel makes a good deodorant also, and it makes a passable **aftershave** too. Simply drench a cotton ball in the alcohol or witch hazel and swab on your skin. Let it dry before you put clothing on and you're good to go.

Deodorant is not the same as antiperspirant. (Antiperspirant has aluminum in it, which is what keeps you from sweating…but that is also the ingredient in antiperspirant that concerns some people.) Deodorant won't keep you from sweating, but it will help you smell fresher.

You can't keep trouble from coming, but you needn't give it a chair to sit on.
—AMISH PROVERB

Notes:

58

Baking soda, cornstarch, and arrowroot powder, mixed together make an excellent **deodorant**. (Baking soda is irritating on some types of sensitive skin, so go easy at first to see how you react. You can skip that ingredient entirely.) This can be a dry-only option, but you can also include a little coconut oil if you like.

- Mix together roughly equal parts of baking soda, cornstarch, and arrowroot powder and then use a powder puff or cotton ball to lightly dab on your underarms.

- Rub a small amount of coconut oil on your underarms and then, using the powder puff or cotton ball, lightly dab on the mixed dry ingredients. (Use the type of coconut oil that is solid at room temperature and quickly rub it into your skin as the coconut oil tends to liquefy at about 75 degrees.)

- For a third option, make a thick paste with the coconut oil and dry mixture. Work quickly so the coconut oil doesn't liquefy when it comes in contact with your body heat. Store the deodorant in a small, clean container. Scoop out a pea-sized amount and then rub it into your underarm and then repeat for the other side. If your home is cool enough you can keep it in a cupboard, but if it seems too soft, consider storing it in the fridge.

- If you're in a hurry, you can simply mix together equal parts baking soda and cornstarch and use a powder puff or cotton balls to dab the powder onto your skin. And if you add a few drops of an essential oil such as lavender, you'll smell nice—and lavender is antibacterial too.

PERSONAL CARE

Notes:

59

Summer means spending time outdoors, and chances are that someone is more than likely going to get **stung by a bee** or **yellow jacket**. Yellow jacket stings seem to be especially painful, and they often swell up and cause great discomfort to the person unlucky enough to get stung.

But if you have a penny and a Band-Aid or some Scotch tape or masking tape (even duct tape would work in a pinch), you have an easy, quick, and effective fix for the discomfort and swelling.

When someone gets stung, wash and dry a penny (although if there's no place to clean a penny, you can spit on it and rub it dry on your clothing or just use it as is). Place the penny on the sting and tape it in place with the Band-Aid. That's all there is to it.

Keep the penny taped on for several hours or overnight if possible (hard to do with little ones, I know, but be persistent), and when you take it off you'll notice there's no swelling. Our family has used this remedy on young and old alike, even a nine-month-old baby who was stung by a yellow jacket, and it always works.

PERSONAL CARE

Notes:

60

Are your leather shoes scuffed and unsightly? There is a simple way to bring back the luster and health of old leather. **Shine your shoes** inexpensively and easily by using any kind of food-grade oil (think canola or olive). Simply wipe on a bit of the oil using a clean, soft rag, let it set for about five minutes, and then wipe off any excess that hasn't soaked into the leather. I personally use sesame oil for my brown and black leather shoes because sesame oil is dark in color and I think it works better than the lighter oils.

Of course, if your leather has been sadly neglected for some time, you will need to repeat this process several times—perhaps once a week or so, or whenever the leather begins to look dry and unconditioned again.

Peace rules the day when Christ rules the mind.
—AMISH PROVERB

Notes:

61

A homemade **exfoliating scrub** can really smooth and soften your skin. My personal favorite uses coffee, sugar, and several other delicious ingredients.

½ cup coconut oil (use cold-pressed oil made from coconut meat)
1 tsp. honey
1 tsp. vanilla
1 cup sugar (I like to use organic or raw sugar because it is a bit coarser than regular granulated)
1 cup ground coffee, medium grind (not used)

Coconut oil liquefies above about 75 degrees, so if it's solid, heat it gently just until liquefied. You can do this in a double boiler or microwave. Remove from heat and pour the oil into a medium-size mixing bowl. Immediately add the honey and vanilla and stir to mix and melt the honey. Set the oil mixture aside until it's cooled. (It won't yet be re-solidified, but it will be cool to the touch.)

Add the sugar to the cooled oil and mix thoroughly. Next, add the coffee grounds and mix thoroughly again.

Store in wide-mouth half-pint canning jars (it takes about three of them) or other suitable containers. Refrigerate the jars not currently in use, especially if the temperature is hot, so the scrub doesn't liquefy.

To use: Scoop out a small amount onto your fingers and massage into your skin and then rinse thoroughly. This exfoliating scrub will leave your skin feeling smooth and soft. In fact, I even use it on my face.

PERSONAL CARE

Notes:

62

Gardening is a pleasure for many of us, but **dirty, stained hands and fingernails** are often a result of tending our flowers and veggies. Of course, the simple answer is to wear gardening gloves, but if you're like me, there are many times when gloves just plain get in the way. So instead, try these ideas.

- Before heading outside, scrape your fingernails across a bar of soap. The soap will get under your nails and be easier to scrub clean afterward.

- Add a spoonful of sugar when you wash your hands and scrub vigorously. The sugar acts as an exfoliator and gets rid of dirt and stains. (Sugar works great on grease too.)

- First wash your hands and then soak your fingernails in hydrogen peroxide for several minutes to bleach away plant stains. Rinse when clean.

- Use a small paper clip to clean under your fingernails. The paper clip dislodges the dirt but doesn't poke your skin like scissors or a knife might.

- Make a pumice cleanser by mixing together ½ cup mason's sand, ⅛ cup pumice powder, and enough glycerin to moisten and hold the ingredients together. Store in a glass jar with a tight-fitting lid. Wet your hands and scrub with 1 tablespoon of the pumice mixture.

PERSONAL CARE

Notes:

63

Rose hip tea is a great **vitamin C immune system booster**. Make this preparation throughout the winter months, and you'll stave off most of the winter colds and flu that strike.

- Combine 4 rounded teaspoons cut and sifted rose hips (ground in a spice mill or not) or 4 tablespoons whole dried rose hips with 4 cups of water in a nonreactive saucepan (such as stainless steel). Cover, bring to a boil, and then simmer for 5 minutes.

- Alternatively, place fresh or crushed dried rose hips in a warmed teapot, pour boiling water over them, and steep, covered, for 10 minutes.

- Strain the tea and sweeten if desired. Serve immediately or cool and refrigerate, covered, for as long as 3 days.

It's so easy to harvest your own rose hips. Almost all roses produce hips, which form after blooming, but the best hips form on rugosa roses, so if you plan to grow your own, look into this variety. Where I live, rugosas are ubiquitous. They thrive on neglected homesteads, in fields, and even along the side of many roads, so it's easy to pick large quantities even if you don't have a rose garden.

Harvest hips after the first frost for the sweetest taste. They will be somewhat firm and red or orange in color. Wash the hips and then slice or cut open (scissors work well for this) and remove the seeds. Place the open hips in a warm, dry place and leave them until they shrivel up and dry. You can store your rose hips in the refrigerator or freezer.

Notes:

64

Mint tea is delicious and makes a great remedy for **upset** and **gassy stomachs**—especially in instances of overeating or eating excessively rich foods. It can also help with **morning sickness** when you are expecting.

Boil 1 cup water and then add 2 teaspoons fresh or 1 teaspoon dried spearmint or peppermint leaves. Cover and let steep for 10 minutes. Drink as is, or pour over ice for a refreshing iced tea.

Mint is an easy perennial plant to grow and harvest. In fact, it can be invasive in many growing zones, so you may want to tame it a bit by growing your mint in a large pot. You can simply go outside and snip what you need, but it's a good idea to harvest your plants in the late summer so you have a steady supply for tea all winter long. Simply cut back the plant to about 6 inches, remove the leaves from the stems, and dry them. The plant needs to put out a bit of new growth before winter sets in, and it will start growing in earnest next spring. When you go shopping for your plants, check out the many different kinds that are available. Besides peppermint and spearmint, you can also find chocolate mint (delightful!), orange mint, apple mint, and pineapple mint, to name just a few.

PERSONAL CARE

Notes:

65

Eye strain, allergies, conjunctivitis, and the common cold can cause **red, swollen eyes**. You can remedy this by preparing a boric acid eye wash. It's simple to prepare and quite effective. You'll need:

1 pint water
⅛ tsp. medicinal grade boric acid
coffee filter or cheesecloth
eye cup, small bowl, or eye dropper

Boil the water for 10 minutes. Measure out 1 cup of the sterilized water and add the boric acid. Stir to mix thoroughly. Strain the mixture through a coffee filter or cheesecloth that has been folded several times. Allow the strained mixture to cool.

To use: Fill a sterilized eye cup or small bowl with the wash and then submerge the affected eye(s) completely. Blink and roll your eyes and keep submerged for 1 minute. If using an eye dropper, fill the dropper with liquid. Tilt your head back and slowly squeeze the wash into your eye, blinking and rolling your eye as you do so. Repeat several times.

Notes:

66

Hiccups can be irritating, and getting rid of them can be challenging. But here are a few tried-and-true ideas.

- Eat a spoonful of sugar. Let the sugar rest in the back of your mouth for a few seconds before swallowing.

- Plug your ears and drink a glass of water using a straw.

- Drink half a spoonful of dill pickle juice or vinegar every 10 seconds until hiccups are gone.

- Drink water from the backside of the glass rim.

*It's easier to dodge responsibility
than to dodge the results.*
—AMISH PROVERB

Notes:

67

If you have youngsters in your life, chances are good that at least one of them will get **chewing gum** stuck in their hair. You can always reach for scissors to cut the gum out, but before you do, try these solutions first.

- Apply vegetable oil liberally on the gum and the surrounding hair. Leave the oil on for several minutes and then gently comb to release strands. It's best to work from the edges toward the center. You'll want to release just a few strands at a time. When the gum is entirely gone, shampoo the hair. (You may need to shampoo twice in order to remove all of the oil.)

- Crack open an egg and separate the white from the yolk. Massage the egg white into the affected hair, going beyond the gum itself. Make sure you saturate the entire area. Leave the egg white on the hair for 10 minutes and then you should be able to just shampoo the hair to get the gum out.

Notes:

68

Homemade **tooth cleaner** and **whitener** couldn't be easier to make. Mix together equal parts crushed dried sage leaves, baking soda, and salt.

To use: Wet your toothbrush and then scoop up some of the cleaner. Use a circular motion to brush your teeth and gums and then rinse well.

Note: Powder the sage instead of using it in leaf form.

Worry is like a rocking chair. It gives you something to do but gets you nowhere.

—AMISH PROVERB

Notes:

Blackheads and **acne** happen, and they are not an indicator of a lack of personal hygiene. In fact, vigorously scrubbing your face can actually exacerbate the problem because you are inadvertently causing your pores to produce more oil to replace what you have industriously scrubbed away. But there are some homemade solutions to help you get rid of unwanted blemishes.

- Make a paste using nutmeg and buttermilk. The amounts you use aren't critical—just add enough buttermilk to some nutmeg until you have a thin paste. Gently wash your face with soap and water and then massage the buttermilk on the areas that are affected for several minutes. Rinse with tepid water and pat your skin dry.

- Mix baking soda and water, using as much of each as you need to produce a paste. Gently wash your face with soap and water and then massage the paste on the affected areas. Allow the paste to stay on your face until dry and crumbly and then rinse with tepid water and pat your skin dry.

- Wash your face with soap and water and then gently massage your wet skin with a paste made from toothpaste and table or sea salt. Rinse and pat dry.

- Honey alone is great to use on your skin to help keep future blackheads from appearing. Honey is an antibacterial agent, and it also puts an oxygen barrier on your skin so the oil in your pores doesn't oxidize and turn black. Dab a little on your skin. Leaving this for several hours or longer will increase the honey's therapeutic effects.

PERSONAL CARE

Notes:

SALVES, OINTMENTS, TONICS, AND BALMS

They provided them with clothes and sandals,
food and drink, and healing balm.

2 CHRONICLES 28:15

Heavenly Father, You provide all that we need
and I am grateful. I ask that You would help me
to be careful to distinguish between needs and
wants. I know You own the cattle on a thousand
hills. Everything in the universe comes from Your
hand, and You are loving and generous. My desire
is to always be in Your will so I don't wander off
the path You have set before me. Teach me, Lord,
to be content in every instance of my life.
In Jesus' name, amen.

70

Comfrey—also known as bone knit—works wonders on **bruises, cuts, strains,** and **sprains**. Making **comfrey salve** is easy.

1 cup dried comfrey leaves
1½ cups olive oil
4 tsp. grated beeswax

Scald a clean quart jar and lid to sterilize. Add the dried comfrey leaves to the jar and then pour the olive oil over them and cover tightly. Set the jar in a cool, dark place (a cupboard works well) for about two weeks.

At the end of the two weeks, pour the infused oil and comfrey leaves into a nonreactive saucepan (such as stainless steel) and gently warm the oil. You want to get it hot enough so that the beeswax will melt (which you will add in the next step), but not hot enough to boil. Strain the hot oil through several layers of fine mesh cheesecloth and then discard the comfrey leaves. Add the beeswax to the warm oil and stir until the beeswax is completely melted (a bamboo grilling skewer works well for this and can be thrown away when you are finished). Pour the comfrey salve into scalded containers that have tight-fitting lids (wide-mouth half-pint canning jars work well) and allow the salve to cool completely and set up before covering with the lids.

Store in a cool, dark place, such as a cupboard or in the refrigerator, and rub onto the affected area as needed.

SALVES, OINTMENTS, TONICS, AND BALMS

Notes:

71

Did you know that honey has antibacterial, wound-healing, anti-microbial, and anti-inflammatory qualities? Because of these characteristics, honey is a great choice for **healing cuts** and **scratches**.

Here's an old-time recipe for **honey-comfrey salve**:

½ cup dried comfrey leaves
1 cup honey

Scald a clean jar that has a tight-fitting lid and then put the dried comfrey leaves into the jar. Heat the honey so it will pour easily over the comfrey leaves. Place the lid on the jar and set it in a cool, dark place for a week so the comfrey infuses the honey. At the end of the week, heat the honey and then strain it through a fine mesh screen, discarding the comfrey leaves. To store the honey-comfrey salve, scald a glass container (a wide-mouth canning jar works well) and pour the strained honey into the jar. Keep it covered tightly and set the jar in a cool, dark place. Make sure you mark the jar so it won't be mistaken for plain honey!

To use: First clean the wound and then smear the honey-comfrey salve on the wound. It will be sticky, so use the back of a spoon or a butter knife to apply and then loosely cover the wound with gauze. Change the dressing several times a day, adding another layer of the salve each time.

SALVES, OINTMENTS, TONICS, AND BALMS

Notes:

72

One of the simplest and oldest recipes for healing **cuts and bruises** uses comfrey and lard. The recipe for **comfrey salve** is not a hard and fast one, so use the directions that follow as a guideline.

In the top of a double boiler, melt 1-2 cups lard on as low of a heat setting as possible (this may take a while). You never want the lard to boil. Cut up or tear fresh, clean comfrey leaves and rub them to bruise the leaves. Add the comfrey—approximately 1 cup or a bit more—to the lard and allow the mixture to simmer for 30 minutes to one hour. Strain the leaves out of the lard using a fine mesh screen or a double layer of cheesecloth and discard the leaves. Pour the strained salve into scalded containers that have tight-fitting lids (wide-mouth half-pint canning jars work well) and allow the salve to cool completely and solidify before covering with the lids.

Store in a cool, dark place, such as a cupboard or the refrigerator, and rub onto the affected area as needed.

SALVES, OINTMENTS, TONICS, AND BALMS

Let's not overlook life's small joys
while looking for the big ones.

—Amish proverb

Notes:

73

Dry skin can be a problem, especially in winter. What you need is a daily dose of **soothing lotion**. In the old days, cooks would often rub a bit of vegetable oil, lard, or shortening into their hands to keep their skin soft and smooth. That's still an option, of course, but here's a slightly more refined alternative to remedy **dry, itchy skin.**

½ cup vegetable or olive oil
½ cup coconut oil (or ¼ cup cocoa butter and ¼ cup coconut oil)
½ cup beeswax, finely grated (measure grated and not packed
    down)
1 pint canning jar

Combine the oils and beeswax in the canning jar. Place the jar in a saucepan and add enough water until it comes at least halfway up the side of the canning jar. Be careful not to get water in the jar (water and oil do not mix). Turn the heat on medium-low and stir while the beeswax and oils melt together. When the mixture is fully lique-fied, remove the jar from the saucepan using hot pads and place in the refrigerator (on another hot pad) to cool and thicken. (Canning jars are made of tempered glass so they can go directly into the refrigerator.) Stir the balm every 15 minutes for at least one hour. (I use a timer so I don't forget.)

Because the ingredients are so minimal, this soothing cream can be used on your face too. A little goes a long way!

Notes:

74

Are **chapped lips** bothering you? Cold and windy winter weather can wreak havoc on sensitive skin. This **lip balm** is the perfect antidote, and the addition of honey gives it an antibacterial boost. Plus, it tastes great!

½ cup almond or other vegetable oil, such as olive or coconut oil
4 T. finely grated beeswax
2 tsp. honey
1 tsp. vanilla (optional)

Place the oil and beeswax in a small saucepan and heat on low to medium-low until the beeswax melts. Remove from the burner and add the honey and vanilla. Stir well. Immediately pour into clean containers. The smaller the container, the better—you want to be able to easily run your finger over the top to get to the lip balm and apply it without having to dig it out with a fingernail. Don't close the top of the container until the lip balm has cooled completely and set up.

*A smile is such a powerful weapon
you can even break ice with it.*

—AMISH PROVERB

SALVES, OINTMENTS,
TONICS, AND BALMS

Notes:

75

Skin rashes are irritating, but **calendula flower salve** can soothe your rash. And it's so gentle you can even use it on a baby's skin.

1 cup olive oil infused with dried calendula flowers (see instructions below for how to make this)
¼ cup finely grated beeswax

To make infused oil: In a saucepan or double boiler, pour in olive oil and ½ cup dried calendula flowers. Heat on low for about 2 hours, stirring occasionally. Do not boil. Strain out the flowers using a fine mesh screen or several layers of cheesecloth. You can use immediately or store the infused oil in a sterilized glass jar with a tight-fitting lid.

To make calendula salve: In a medium saucepan, melt the beeswax with the infused oil, stirring until the beeswax is completely melted. Pour the salve into a sterilized jar and cool completely before covering with a lid. Store in a cool, dark area, such as your pantry or a bathroom cabinet.

To use: Gently rub a small amount of salve onto the affected area. This is so gentle that you can use it on most sensitive skin types. And if you want to get a bit fancy, after you remove the salve from the stove, stir in about 10 drops of lavender essential oil for a nice scent.

SALVES, OINTMENTS, TONICS, AND BALMS

Notes:

Black drawing salve is just the thing for drawing out splinters, thorns, and tiny pieces of glass that get stuck in your skin. It also works to draw out the infection in insect bites and boils. You can buy black drawing salve at most Amish stores because it's used so often, but here's a basic recipe you can make yourself.

6 T. olive oil infused with plantain leaves or calendula flowers (see below)
2 T. castor oil
2 tsp. finely grated beeswax
1 T. honey
3 tsp. activated charcoal
3 tsp. bentonite or Kaolin clay

To infuse your olive oil, place about ½ cup calendula flowers or torn plantain leaves in a small saucepan. Add a cup of olive oil and warm it on very low heat for 2-3 hours, stirring occasionally. When the oil is infused, strain out the plant matter and store the oil in a cool, dark area until needed.

Now, to make the black drawing salve. Using a clean can or a small canning jar, mix together the oils and beeswax and place the jar in a saucepan. Add enough water so that it comes to about halfway up the side of the jar or can. (Be careful that you don't get any water into the jar.) Heat on low to medium-low, stirring often, until the beeswax has completely melted. Using hot pads, remove the jar from the saucepan and promptly stir in the honey, charcoal, and clay. Store the drawing

SALVES, OINTMENTS, TONICS, AND BALMS

Notes:

salve in a glass container that has a tight-fitting lid and keep it in a cool, dry area, such as a bathroom cabinet or kitchen cupboard.

To use: Daub the salve onto the affected area and then cover with gauze or a large bandage. Keep it on for at least several hours or overnight. Repeat if necessary until the foreign object has been drawn out or the bite or sting has begun healing and no longer throbs.

77

There's nothing exotic about this tried-and-true remedy, but eating a fresh **garlic clove** daily really works to keep a person healthy. This immune system tonic is especially effective during the winter months when cold and flu season is at its height. You can actually buy garlic in capsule form these days, but long before garlic supplements were available, families practiced "a clove a day to keep the doctor away." In fact, garlic was eaten by Greek and Roman soldiers before they headed out to fight their battles because they believed it would give them strength and endurance. Today, many folks are convinced that garlic is also good for your heart, reduces high blood pressure, makes for stronger bones and healthier connective tissues, lowers cholesterol, and works as a splendid antioxidant.

To get the most benefit from your daily dose of garlic, start with a whole clove. Peel the garlic and then mince or smash it. Wait for several minutes to release all of the juices and then eat it. You can find refrigerated minced garlic in the produce aisle of many grocery stores, but resist the urge to buy the minced garlic and instead use a freshly prepared garlic clove so you get the full health benefits.

Notes:

Of course, there's a downside to the daily use of garlic for some people. The smell of garlic can be a bother, but if you eat an apple or drink a glass of milk (whole milk works better than low-fat or skim milk) after ingesting the garlic you should find that your family and friends won't keel over when you open your mouth to say hello.

78

Dandelion salad has been a well-loved spring tonic for generations. In early spring Amish children forage for dandelion greens to make a tasty salad that is rumored to cleanse the blood, which has turned sluggish from the long winter. And after months of making meals from your winter pantry, a fresh garden salad made from the spicy dandelion will be a welcome taste.

You can grow dandelion greens in your vegetable garden, but it's just as easy to simply go outside and gather a mess of greens growing wild in your yard. You can pull up entire plants (you'll still need to cut the leaves from the root) or simply cut some of the leaves from the plant and leave the rest to keep growing for a later harvest. Clean the greens well and place them on a towel to dry. Then you can tear them into bite-sized pieces and drizzle with your favorite dressing.

Here's a very basic oil-and-vinegar salad dressing:

1 cup oil
½ cup vinegar (experiment with different vinegars, such as cider or balsamic)
salt and pepper to taste
herbs and spices of your choice (optional)

SALVES, OINTMENTS, TONICS, AND BALMS

Notes:

Put all of the ingredients in a jar with a tight-fitting lid and shake to blend. The dressing will separate, but just shake again right before using. However, if you add a pinch of dried mustard powder, your dressing won't separate quite as readily because mustard powder works as an emulsifier.

You can eat dandelion salad plain or add in whatever pleases your taste buds. In our family, we sometimes enjoy including a can of drained mandarin oranges, bacon bits, cheddar cheese chunks, or hard boiled eggs.

79

If you suffer from **toenail fungus**, try soaking your feet in **Listerine** mouthwash, or a combination of equal parts Listerine and white vinegar. This is quite effective, but you'll need to soak for 20 minutes a day until your toenails have completely regrown, which can take about 9-12 months, so you'll have to practice patience and keep at it consistently. Use fresh mixture each day. Also, remember to disinfect toenail clippers and scissors after every use so you don't keep reinfecting your nails, and stay away from using nail polish on the infected nails.

You can further help by wearing natural fiber socks and sprinkling antifungal powders inside your shoes or socks before putting them on in the morning.

There's really no quick cure for getting rid of toenail fungus, so be prepared to stick with it until your nails are once again healthy and pink.

Notes:

80

Mentholatum ointment and **Vicks VapoRub** are both great choices for getting rid of **nail fungus**. Use a Q-tip or your fingertip to rub the ointment onto your infected nail(s). Do this morning and evening until the nail has completely regrown, about 9-12 months. Never re-dip your finger or Q-tip into the jar of ointment once you have touched the nail so you don't spread the fungus.

Also, if you use your fingers to apply the medicine, wash your hands well with lots of soap and warm water as soon as you're finished. Use a paper towel to dry your hands and then throw it away.

*You cannot do everything at once, but you
can do something at once.*

—Amish proverb

SALVES, OINTMENTS,
TONICS, AND BALMS

Notes:

81

When you accidentally **burn** your hand, **cut** a finger, or get a minor **sunburn**, reach for the **aloe vera** plant. It's an easy-to-grow succulent that thrives in outdoor gardens in hardiness zones 9 and 10. But because many of us live in colder growing zones, you'll need to bring your plant indoors during the winter months. You can treat aloe vera like a houseplant, but if you take the pot outside during warm summers, it will grow larger and possibly even flower.

To use: Simply cut off a bit of thick leaf, slice it open along its length to expose the interior, and rub the antibacterial gel that oozes out onto the affected area. Keep an aloe vera plant on a sunny windowsill in your kitchen, where minor burns and cuts often seem to happen. Aloe vera gel is also effective in relieving the itch from insect bites and stings.

The lowest ebb is the turn of the tide.

—Amish proverb

SALVES, OINTMENTS, TONICS, AND BALMS

Notes:

82

It's hard to not scratch when you are experiencing **itchy skin** from poison oak, poison ivy, eczema, or insect bites, but you *can* relieve the itch with these home remedies.

- Grind up oatmeal and make a paste by adding some water. Apply the paste to your affected skin and allow it to dry completely. You can gently soak the oatmeal in cool water when you wish to remove it. The paste will help to draw out the toxins and reduce the pain and itch.

- You can also take an oatmeal bath. Grind some oatmeal and pour it into the water coming out of the faucet as you're filling the tub. (Use warm, not hot, water.) Swish the water around periodically to disperse the oatmeal and then relax in the tub for 20-25 minutes.

- You can also place oatmeal in a bag made of muslin or cheesecloth and let the water from the faucet run over the bag as you fill the tub. Periodically squeeze the bag as the tub is filling. When you are bathing, you can use the bag (still filled with the oatmeal) to gently scrub your skin.

SALVES, OINTMENTS, TONICS, AND BALMS

Notes:

83

Mosquito bites seem to be a fact of life in the summer months, and the swelling and itching from them can be irritating. But here are some tried-and-true home remedies to kick the itch.

- Make a paste with baking soda and cool water and apply to the bite. Leave it on until the itching stops, and reapply as necessary.
- Dab some toothpaste on the bite. The mint in the toothpaste helps to immediately soothe the area.
- Break off a bit of an aloe vera leaf, split it open, and wipe the gel onto the affected area. Let it dry.
- Break open an egg and, using a cotton ball or small cloth (we've even used paper towels), wipe the egg white onto the mosquito bite. Let it dry on your skin.

Enthusiam is contagious, and so is the lack of it.
—AMISH PROVERB

Notes:

SLEEP ISSUES, ANXIETY, STRESS, AND NERVOUS TENSION

In peace I will lie down and sleep,
for you alone, LORD,
make me dwell in safety.

PSALM 4:8

Heavenly Father, sometimes life can feel overwhelming.
It's at these times, Lord, that I'll do well to remember that
You are always with me and I'm not going through these
tough spots alone. Thank You for that! During difficult
times, bring to my mind Your Word. Remind me to pray.
Cause me to offer up the sacrifice of praise, for surely
the darkness that seems to surround me will flee when
encompassed by Your light. I know I will find peace when
I seek Your face, so "because [God] bends down to listen, I
will pray as long as I have breath!" (Psalm 116:2 NLT).
In Jesus' name, amen.

84

Try valerian root tea when you are **nervous** or **can't sleep**. Valerian has been used for generations to help a person get to sleep and stay asleep longer. You can grow and dry your own, but dried valerian root is so widely available it's almost not worth the effort. Still, if you choose to grow this perennial plant, harvest the roots in the second year. Wash the roots well to remove all traces of dirt and small rocks. To dry the roots, first cut them into similar sized pieces and lay them out with space between each piece in a cool, shady place for about 10 days. (I use an interior closet in my home.) Every day, turn the roots so they have good air circulation all around.

To use: Make a tea by steeping 1 teaspoon of dried valerian root for 10 minutes in a cup of boiling water. Strain out the root, add honey to taste, and drink about an hour before bedtime.

Keep in mind that it may take a week or two to notice the improvement in your sleep, so be patient.

SLEEP ISSUES
AND STRESS

Notes:

85

Anxiety can be relieved by drinking tea made from lemon balm. Pour a cup of boiling water over 5 fresh leaves (or 1 teaspoon dried) and let it steep for 5 minutes. Strain and add honey if desired. Drink a cup several times a day when you are feeling stressed.

You can also make tea using a teaspoon each of lemon balm, chamomile, and peppermint steeped for 10 minutes in a quart of boiling water. Strain out the herbs and drink it warm or iced, with or without honey. Soothing and tasty!

Lemon balm, chamomile, and peppermint are all easy-to-grow herbs that can thrive in many gardening climates. But beware—peppermint and lemon balm (or any plant in the mint family) can become invasive, so it may be better to grow these plants in a large pot. Chamomile is either a freely self-sowing annual or perennial, depending on the variety. Either can be used for tea.

Every child has the right to be well fed and well led.

—AMISH PROVERB

SLEEP ISSUES
AND STRESS

Notes:

86

For **mild depression** and **achy muscles,** Saint-John's-wort will help. (I was told years ago by an older woman that it's called Saint-John's-wort because the flowers bloom around June 24, which was the apostle's birthday.) Saint-John's-wort is an easy-to-grow perennial plant with pretty, bright yellow flowers that bloom profusely. In fact, it's the flowers that are harvested to make tea or used in massage oil. Dry the flowers in the shade outside or use a dehydrator set on a low heat. Make sure they are completely dry before storing.

- To make tea, pour a cup of boiling water over a teaspoon of the dried herb and allow it to steep for about 5 minutes before straining. Drink up to 3 cups per day for mild depression.

- For achy muscles, Saint-John's-wort-infused olive oil massaged into the skin near sore muscles will relieve pain. To make, gather fresh Saint-John's-wort flowers and put them in a glass jar that has been scalded to sanitize it. (Canning jars work well for this.) Pour olive oil into the jar, making sure the flowers are completely covered. Place in the sun for 2 or 3 weeks. As the oil infuses, it will turn red. (This is supposed to happen, so don't be alarmed.) When you're ready to store the oil, strain it into another scalded jar and keep it covered tightly in a dark place or use a dark glass jar if you have one. Use the oil to massage aching joints and muscles as well as for back pain.

SLEEP ISSUES AND STRESS

Notes:

87

Depression affects more than 350 million people around the world, according to a recent report issued by the World Health Organization (www.who.int/mediacentre/factsheets/fs369/en/). Sadly, only about a third of the people who suffer from depression seek treatment. There are many prescription treatments available, but if your depression is mild and not chronic, you might try the following natural remedies to elevate your mood.

- *Exercise* releases endorphins and can help you feel happier. Brisk walking, bike riding, or jogging are good exercises when you have depression. But any kind of exercise is better than none at all. Just keep in mind that if you are having trouble sleeping at night, don't exercise too late in the day.

- *Light therapy* works wonders, especially for those of us who suffer from seasonal affective disorder, or SAD. There are special light boxes you can purchase, but it's also possible to use a full spectrum lightbulb in a regular lamp you can sit close to. Don't stare at the light, but do let it shine on your skin. Start with about 15 minutes each day and see if you get relief. Some people need as much as two hours a day under those special bulbs. I tend to get blue during the short, dark days of winter, so I keep a special bulb in the floor lamp where I read or knit in the evening as well as a special bulb in my desk lamp where I work during the day.

SLEEP ISSUES AND STRESS

Notes:

- *Support or interest groups* can help you feel better. Support groups aren't as popular as they once were, so if you can't find one you're comfortable with near you, try joining a group that shares an interest that you have or would like to know more about. It could be a reading group, a mall walking group, or a photography class, to name some examples.

- *Fish oil* is also quite helpful. Research shows that populations that consume foods high in Omega-3 fatty acids (such as is found in salmon, tuna, mackerel, and sardines) have a lower incidence of depression. You would have to eat fish pretty much daily in order to relieve your depression, so taking a supplement may be a wiser (and easier and cheaper) choice. You can buy fish oil in gelatin capsules, but I take my daily dose by the tablespoon. Yes, it's oily, but the brand I buy adds lemon, and that helps.

- *Saint-John's-wort* is a great old-time remedy for depression. You can get it anywhere, it's inexpensive, and it works.

- *SAM-e* (S-adenosylmethionine) is made in your body from a reaction of an essential amino acid and a molecule that carries energy, and it's found in all of your living cells. You can't make SAM-e at home, but you can buy it as a supplement in most stores, including big box stores. It usually comes in 200- or 400-milligram tablets. You can start by taking 200 milligrams daily, but if you don't begin to feel better after a week or so, you can increase the dose (in steps) to as high as 1600 milligrams daily. Usually 800 milligrams is plenty. Also, SAM-e seems to work better if you take a vitamin B-complex tablet along with it.

Notes:

88

Almost everyone at one time or another has a **difficult time sleeping**. Hops can help.

- Steep a teaspoon of hops (called strobiles) in one cup of hot water for 5 minutes, add some honey, and drink about 30 minutes before bedtime.

- Place a cup of dried hops into a sachet bag (you can easily make one yourself) that has a drawstring closure that can be pulled tight. Place the sachet under your pillow to help you relax and get a good night's sleep.

You can actually grow your own hops, and it's enjoyable for many to do so. Hops are perennial, and each growing season the vine starts from the crown and grows straight up on a sturdy string or wire that the gardener furnishes. You can almost sit and watch these vines grow—they reach as high as 25-30 feet by the end of the growing season.

Christ does not leave a soul when joys and comforts leave it.

—Amish proverb

SLEEP ISSUES
AND STRESS

Notes:

89

If you have **young children**, you are likely to have **problems getting them to sleep**. To make matters even more difficult, there are many theories about how to successfully negotiate bedtime with your toddler, with devotees of each theory solidly lined up according to their strong opinions. What about the family bed? Is white noise beneficial? Can my toddler have a pacifier or bottle to help her fall asleep? Should I allow him to play quietly in his bed before falling asleep? Those questions and more can plague parents, who are often frustrated and sleep deprived and just want some answers. As much as I'd love to be able to give you, say, 5 Steps to a Successful Bedtime, there just isn't one right answer. But here are some things to keep in mind.

- *Stay calm and consistent.* No matter how resistant your toddler is to actually going to bed and falling asleep, your calm voice and consistent routine will help immeasurably.

- *Follow a bedtime routine.* Do the same things each night as your child gets ready for bed, at the same time and in the same order. This will help your child know what to expect and will calm her.

- *Be prepared.* Think through your child's reasonable needs and desires and make them a part of the nightly routine. For instance, have them go potty one more time, place a glass of water on the nightstand, and make sure their special blanket or stuffed toy is at hand. Spend some minutes hugging and speaking quietly. Turn on the

Notes:

night-light and check under the bed and in all corners for "monsters" if your child is fearful.

- *Let your child decide between two choices.* Don't leave your questions open ended. You could ask, "Would you like to wear your princess pajamas or your purple pajamas?" "Would you rather read *Go, Dog. Go!* or *Goodnight Moon*?"

- *Allow one extra request.* Little ones like to feel as though they got something extra, but you know that you both gain because you permitted one—and only one—extra request.

- *Tell your child you will come back in to check on him in 5 minutes.* Then do it. You can do this several times, but add a bit of time between subsequent visits.

- *Keep your home quiet.* You want your little one to fall asleep without worrying she's missing out on what's going on beyond her bedroom door.

Parents can be sleep deprived for several years as their toddlers grow. It's hard on moms and dads, but these years will indeed end. In fact, one day the tables will be turned, and you'll be wondering how to get your teen to wake up.

SLEEP ISSUES
AND STRESS

Notes:

WOMEN'S
HEALTH

I also want the women to dress modestly,
with decency and propriety, adorning themselves,
not with elaborate hairstyles or gold
or pearls or expensive clothes,
but with good deeds, appropriate for women
who profess to worship God.

1 Timothy 2:9-10

Heavenly Father, how blessed I am to be counted as one
of Your daughters! Help me to dress and carry myself in
such a way that I never bring disgrace to You. Instead,
Lord, I want to be a strong witness to Your saving grace.
So remind me often that the best adornment I can hope
to have is a servant's heart, a willing and helpful attitude,
and a constant yearning to know You more. May it be
said of me that when people see me, they see You as well.
In Jesus' name, amen.

90

Although anyone can get a **bladder infection** (also called a **urinary tract infection** or **UTI**), women are more prone to them than men. Here are some home remedies that will help when you feel a bladder infection coming on.

- Drink plenty of water. The goal is to flush your system so the "bad" bacteria causing your infection don't have as much of a chance to multiply.

- Drink lots of cranberry juice—about 3 tall glasses a day. Make sure it's the real deal and unsweetened. (While sweetening a beverage often makes it more enjoyable, for this remedy it can be counterproductive.) Eating fresh blueberries or drinking blueberry nectar works as well.

- Eat yogurt, the kind that contains live active cultures. The good bacteria found in the yogurt will help keep the bad bacteria produced by your infection at bay. And if you choose to take antibiotics to help get rid of your UTI, eating yogurt is even more important because antibiotics can't differentiate between good (you want those) and bad bacteria and kills both.

- Mix ½ teaspoon baking soda with a glass of water and drink. The baking soda helps to relieve the pain of your bladder infection.

Notes:

- Stir in 1 teaspoon cream of tartar into a cup of warm water, add a spritz of lemon juice, and drink 1-2 cups a day.
- Make parsley tea by placing 2 tablespoons of dried parsley in a cup of hot water. Steep for 5 minutes, strain out the parsley, add a touch of lemon juice if desired (but no sugar), and drink. If you prefer, you can refrigerate the tea and drink it iced.

Some people's idea of housework is to sweep a room with a glance.

—AMISH PROVERB

Notes:

91

Cramps are a monthly struggle for many women, and they can slow us down because we aren't feeling our best. If cramps get you down, try some—or all—of these home remedies.

- Drink milk. The calcium in milk reduces muscle cramping.

- Eat lots of papaya, starting several days before you know you'll be suffering from cramps.

- Take vitamin D3. This is not a water-soluble vitamin, so it's possible you can take too much, but it rarely happens. Consult with your doctor because there's an easy blood test that can tell you what your vitamin D level currently is. The doctor will be able to tell you how much vitamin D3 to take based on your specific level, and you'll probably be surprised at just how much is recommended.

- Use a hot water bottle to relax your muscles.

- Drink raspberry leaf tea, either plain or with a bit of grated fresh ginger root steeped in it as well.

- If you find that your cramps interfere with daily activities and responsibilities, see a doctor.

Notes:

92

Morning sickness is never fun, and suffering from it day after day is just plain tiring. No one really knows what causes morning sickness, and there aren't really any surefire cures, but there are steps you can take to relieve or possibly head off a bout of morning sickness.

- Upon first waking in the morning, reach for a handful of soda crackers or regular potato chips (don't use low-fat or flavored ones). Some women swear by eating them before they even get out of bed, but if the idea of crumbs on your sheets bothers you, try to get some in your stomach just as soon as possible upon rising.

- Drink peppermint or ginger tea. (These teas make great motion sickness remedies as well.)

- Have a cup of warm water, with a splash of lemon, lime, or orange juice added if desired.

- Try a glass of room-temperature, flat ginger ale. It's important to make sure the bubbles have dissipated because they can cause your stomach to make more acid and possibly make you feel worse.

- Chew on fennel seeds. (This also works great for non-pregnancy-related nausea.)

- Eat more small meals when hungry versus two or three large meals. Stay away from spicy foods or foods that cause bloating or gas.

Notes:

- Eat frozen fruit popsicles that are 100 percent fruit. You can even make them yourself. Try freezing orange or grape juice, or crush fresh berries and then strain the juice, adding some of the pulp back into the mixture if that appeals to you.

93

More than likely, you'll be able to continue with your routine diet when **nursing a baby**. But here are some common foods that seem to bother babies on occasion:

- chocolate (sorry about that!)
- strong spices, such as garlic, cinnamon, and chili powder
- citrus fruit and juice
- vegetables that can cause gas, such as broccoli, onions, cabbage, cucumbers, and bell peppers
- fruit with laxative qualities, such as cherries, prune plums, and prune juice

And if your family has any food allergies, stay away from those foods as well. Dairy, wheat, and peanuts are usually at the top of the list.

Notes:

94

White willow bark tea has an ingredient called salicin, which is a natural precursor to the salicylic acid found in aspirin, and acts as a surefire treatment for the pain of **menstrual cramps**. (Note that if you are unable to take aspirin for any reason, you'll want to stay away from this tea.) As an added bonus, this tea works to reduce fevers, is anti-inflammatory, and reduces the pain of headaches and osteo-arthritis. When using white willow bark tea for menstrual cramping, start drinking it a day or two before your period is due. That way, you'll already have it working in your system.

Here's what you'll need to make white willow bark tea:

1-2 tsp. white willow bark
1 cup water
honey or sugar to taste

Place the bark and water in a saucepan (you can double or triple this recipe if you want to make several cups at once) and bring to a boil. Simmer for 10 minutes and then turn off the heat and allow the bark to continue steeping for 30 minutes. Strain the tea and add honey to taste. Drink up to 4 cups daily. It will take some time before you find relief, so be patient. On the plus side, the positive effects of drinking the tea will last a good long while.

Notes:

95

Nursing mother's tea, made from sweet basil leaves, works as a relaxant and promotes the **increase of milk production in nursing mothers.**

To make nursing mother's tea, boil 1 cup water and then add 2 teaspoons shredded or bruised fresh sweet basil leaves or 1 teaspoon dried. Cover and steep for 10 minutes. Strain and drink. You can drink this tea up to three times daily over short periods.

Sweet basil is easy to grow—even indoors on a sunny windowsill. I grow it as an annual, but there have been years when it comes back in the spring because our winter has been unusually mild. An added bonus is that basil helps to repel houseflies (a good reason to grow plants indoors or outside near your entryways), and crushed fresh basil leaves reduces the pain and swelling of insect bites and stings.

Give others a piece of your heart,
not a piece of your mind.

—AMISH PROVERB

Notes:

Nursing mothers sometimes get **mastitis, engorgement,** and **plugged milk ducts,** but problems with infected breasts can happen to any women at any time of life. The symptoms are usually found in only one breast and can include tenderness and swelling, engorgement, redness, fatigue, fever, and flu-like symptoms. In days gone by, women often succumbed to milk fever, but today we have the use of antibiotics to rid our systems of infection—and sometimes this is the only course for success. Certainly, if you've tried home remedies or you have a fever, it's time to immediately head to your doctor's office or urgent care. But there *are* home remedies that can prove successful, especially if you catch it in the beginning stages. And if you use these home remedies in conjunction with your doctor's care, you'll have better success and reduce your symptoms sooner.

- Nurse on the uninfected side first because the baby will satisfy his hunger somewhat and then (you can always hope) he will nurse gentler on the tender, second side. Try to nurse often.

- Gently massage your breasts, imitating your baby's nursing movements. Keep in mind that the milk ducts move toward the nipple, so always massage toward your nipple. Stay away from pumps, as these don't mimic baby's nursing habits and can be hard on sensitive tissue. Pay close attention to any lumps, and work carefully but thoroughly to try to open that plugged duct.

- Take a long shower. Hot, moist heat really helps and soothes. Alternatively, you can soak your breast in a bowl

Notes:

of warm water for about 5 minutes at a time. Gently massage while soaking.

- In between hot showers, place cabbage leaves inside your bra. (This is actually one of the best home remedies, so give it a try.) Cabbage leaves are anti-inflammatory and have a drawing effect to pull out the infection. Go for organic, green cabbage and store the leaves in the refrigerator so that when you go to use them, they are cool (which also helps to reduce inflammation). Wash and dry the leaves and then gently press on their veins to break them down before putting them inside your bra. Keep them in for 2-3 hours before using fresh leaves. Keep in mind, however, that if you're nursing a baby, cabbage leaves will also reduce your milk supply—in fact, using cabbage leaves to help you dry up work great. So if you want to continue nursing your infant, use cabbage for only a day or so until the symptoms begin to wane.

- -

Language may be a vehicle of thought, but in some cases it's just an empty wagon.

—AMISH PROVERB

- -

Notes:

Cracked nipples are another problem that faces nursing moms from time to time, especially in the early going. Cracked nipples can hurt so bad that it's hard to talk yourself into letting your infant latch on, but once the babe gets going, the pain usually lessens, albeit sometimes barely. Try singing as you begin to nurse and consciously relax your shoulders and take deep breaths. Here are some ideas to help you when you are suffering from the pain and rawness of cracked nipples.

- If only one side is affected (or whichever side hurts the most), nurse on the good side first. The baby will satisfy her hunger somewhat and nurse more gently on the second side.

- Consider holding your baby in different positions (such as in a football hold) while she nurses on the tender side.

- Try icing your breast immediately before nursing. It will help anesthetize your nipple and latching on won't be quite as uncomfortable.

- Once or twice a day, mix ½ teaspoon salt in a cup of warm water and soak your breasts for 3-5 minutes. Gently pat dry.

- Purchase medical-grade lanolin (with no other ingredients) and smooth on a thin layer. Lanolin comes from sheep and is fine for nursing babies. But use just a small dab so your baby doesn't reject nursing. Also, if you allow the lanolin to heat to your body temperature, it's easier to apply.

Notes:

98

Yeast infections are irritating, and can become a chronic problem. But if you rarely get such an infection, try these solutions before heading to the doctor's office.

- Wear cotton underwear. Every day. All the time. The natural fiber "breathes" and moisture doesn't stick around.

- Don't scratch! You'll simply make yourself miserable. Try relieving the itch with a cool bath instead.

- Eat live culture yogurt. In fact, yogurt is a good hedge against future yeast problems, so incorporate yogurt into your daily food allotment. Or you can take probiotics, in powder or capsule form. Follow the directions on the container.

- Use a nonprescription antifungal cream and be sure to follow the dosing instructions.

We make a living by what we get, but we make a life by what we give.

—AMISH PROVERB

Notes:

99

Welcome to **menopause and perimenopause**—where hot flashes, night sweats, fuzzy thinking, weight gain, and insomnia move in. This stage in life can last for years, so it's a great idea to know about some handy solutions to alleviate the worst of it.

- *Hot flashes and night sweats.* Dress in layers so you can remove clothing as needed. Try not to stay in overheated rooms. If you work outside of the home, bring a small desk fan to work with you so you can have cooling air movement. Limit caffeine, simple sugars, and spicy foods. Instead, eat plenty of fruits and veggies and drink cold water or juice. Especially eat soy food (beans, tofu, etc.) or drink soy milk daily.

- *Fuzzy thinking.* Fluctuating hormones probably play a part in mild forgetfulness during these years, but reducing your stress level (sometimes hard to do, but work on that), regular exercise, and brain games will help to sharpen your memory.

- *Weight gain.* It seems that the weight creeps up on us throughout perimenopause. Again, this is partly due to hormone fluctuations, but regular exercise can make a big difference. You'll feel good about yourself as you take a positive stand, your stress hormones will be reduced, and you may just see the scale head downward.

Notes:

WOMEN'S HEALTH

- *Insomnia.* Practice a consistent, relaxing, daily bedtime routine. Drink a soothing beverage (such as herbal tea) before closing your eyes. Keep your bedroom cool (a fan can be a boon during warmer weather). Exercise tires you out and thus helps you sleep longer and better, but don't exercise too close to bedtime. Your body needs time to unwind.

You're not what you think you are;
but what you think—you are.

—AMISH PROVERB

Chupp's Herbs & Fabrics

27539 Londick Road
Burr Oak, MI 49030

269-659-3950

Chupp's has dietary supplements, shoes, fabrics, Mutza suits (men's Amish suits), hats, gloves, toys and games, wagons, hand-powered small kitchen appliances, and more. Because they don't have an online presence, you'll have to call or write to request a catalog. More than a hundred pages are jam-packed with products and testimonials, many from satisfied Amish customers. Makes for interesting reading!

Mountain Rose Herbs

www.montainroseherbs.com

This is taken from their website—but I can assure you it's all true because I've shopped with them for years: "Mountain Rose Herbs offers high quality organic bulk herbs, gourmet spices, loose leaf teas, essential oils, herbal extracts, and natural body care ingredients. Our extensive selection includes certified organic, fair trade, ethically wild harvest, and Kosher certified botanical products." I love this store!

Starwest Botanicals

www.starwest-botanicals.com

This online store offers a wide variety of organic and nonorganic bulk herbs, spices, teas, and extracts.

Amazon.com

www.amazon.com

I realize this might seem an odd resource to add to a home remedies book, but over the years I've bought many herbs, spices, and teas from Amazon.com and haven't been disappointed. Their prices are often very good.

501 Time-Saving Tips Every Woman Should Know

Get More Done in Less Time with Less Stress

Would you like some help with your to-do list? Who wouldn't! You'll love these surprisingly quick, easy, and effective ways to complete troublesome tasks in a snap.

- A squeegee or dryer sheet works great for removing pet hair from your furniture and carpet.
- Plain, whole-milk yogurt and a cold-water rinse soothe sunburned skin.
- Add Epsom salts to your watering can to make your garden more productive.
- Put baking soda and vinegar to work removing spots from your old baking pans.
- Use ice cubes to restore your carpet where furniture has left indentations.

You don't have to work harder. Just get smarter—and enjoy the time you'll save.

The Homestyle Amish Kitchen Cookbook

Let a Little Plain Cooking Warm Up Your Life

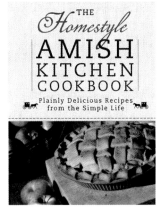

Who doesn't want simplicity in the kitchen?

Most of these delicious, easy-to-make dishes are simplicity itself. The Amish are a productive and busy people. They work hard in the home and on their farms, and they need good, filling food that doesn't require alot of preparation and time. A few basic ingredients, some savory and sweet spices, and and a little love make many of these meals a cook's delight. And if you want something a bit more complex and impressive, those recipes are here for you too.

Along with fascinating tidbits about the Amish way of life, you will find directions for lovely, old-fashioned food such as

- Scrapple
- Honey Oatmeal Bread
- Coffee Beef Stew
- Potato Rivvel Soup
- Snitz and Knepp
- Shoo-Fly Pie

Everything from breakfast to dessert is covered in this celebration of comfort food and family. Hundreds of irresistible options will help you bring the simple life to your own home and kitchen.

The Amish Canning Cookbook

Full Pantry, Full Heart

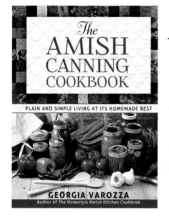

From the author of *The Homestyle Amish Kitchen Cookbook* comes a great new collection of recipes, hints, and Plain wisdom for everyone who loves the idea of preserving fresh, wholesome food. Whether you're a beginning canner or a seasoned cook honing her skills, certified Master Food Preserver Georgia Varozza will show you how to get the very best out of your food. You'll find…

- a short history of canning
- lists of all the tools and supplies you need to get started
- basic instructions for safe canning
- recipes for canning fruit, vegetables, meat, soups, sauces, and more
- guidelines for safely adapting recipes to fit your family's tastes

With its expert advice and warm tones, *The Amish Canning Cookbook* will become a beloved companion to everyone who loves the tradition, frugality, and homestyle flavor of Amish cooking!

To learn more about Harvest House books and
to read sample chapters, visit our website:

www.harvesthousepublishers.com

HARVEST HOUSE PUBLISHERS
EUGENE, OREGON